Queer Fish

Queer Fish

Sarah Giragosian

Dream Horse Press
Aptos, California

Dream Horse Press
Post Office Box 670, Warrenton, Oregon 97146

Printed in the United States of America
Published in 2017 by Dream Horse Press

ISBN 978-1-935716-43-3

Cover artwork:

Strange Fish
by Syra Larkin

http://www.syralarkinart.com/

CONTENTS

For my parents
&
For Elise

I.

"Without the example provided by animals before our eyes, we as a species might be unable to imagine a state beyond the constantly re-created series of delusions in which our existence consists."

—Marcus Bullock, "Watching Eyes, Seeing Dreams, Knowing Lives"

To the Meerkat

This rapt, bandit-eyed mother,
scorpion-diner and foe to cobras,
is not a marauder, but rather
the obverse: upright and slightly simian
on her miniature mongoose legs.

Love is like the sole lookout,
the one who reconnoiters the desert
to keep her clan unharmed. Dear totem,
she telegraphs her cry across the wasteland
if any slinking or winged thing nears,

although her clamant alarm
gives her away. Love's swift and costly here,
and she, banisher of loneliness,
leans in close— dainty nose grazing ear—
to groom another's fur just so.

Lullaby for Cat

I miss you when you are cat
    and I am human,
when you are dreaming
        and I am peeping.
                If I could paddle backwards
        across the wide channel of your sleeping,
I would poke a peephole
    into the bark of your dreaming.
What a relief then to meet
      creature to creature!
We stretch and stray
    with the day. We nose around in the roses
    and sprawl below the bird's eye sheet
        half-flying from the laundry line.
Later we rise and ramble
      through the bird-thickened brambles
      or we tremble against the copper birdbath
      where watery,
            overhead
               birds swim.
In that inverse mirror
    we kiss our shoulders,
      knead our claws on stone,
        and rub at tender wings.
We lap at the bowl of our visions
    and pass the long isthmus of night
      watching the birds hook up
        across fields of telephone wires,
          calling and calling to each other,
while inside the tenants

hang up the landline
or wade into the static air.

I do not miss being human in dreaming,
when you come to me, trilling.

The Decorator Crab,

bedecked with seaweed, polyps, knobs, and buds
of algae, wheels around the shore on legs
like mossy branches while it looks around
for fringe or sponge to hook upon its back.
Its eye for slough is matchless, though the jazz
it wears is mismatched: rosette webs with sand-
encrusted seaweed, scraps of dross and fish
tissue, and hodgepodge bits to hide beneath.
The guise is custom-made, arrayed in such
a way to con and keep its foes away.
There's nothing paltry on its zigzag route,
and every slight anemone or snarl
of string may be desired and conjoined
with it. Eclectic crab, collector flecked
with others, nothing can be drab so long
as objects hold allure as intimates.

What I Mean When I Say I Knew You Long Before We Met

Our storylines were the same.
As girls, we bucked through screen doors
and vaulted out of windows. We galloped away
from our mothers, knocking our hooves through ice
to feel our power. Our bodies then were porous
and promiscuous. We were woodland creatures,
hardly people, and we felt no shame
in small indiscretions. Even being a boy was easy,
nothing more than moulting off a shirt
and uncovering our flat chests.

Our passion grew from our patience.
We tracked the snail in the loam:
we watched it spasm, squinch, and unspool
its wet iridescence across the roots,
muscling its soft body across the hard earth.

We had seen the face of the snail
in the public undulations of its flesh
against the flesh of its mate: a she: a he,
the slurring tongue of its body
sliding across the hermaphroditic soul
of love. They genuflected and leaned back
against their helix shells before they rose,
bodies rhyming, rubbing up against each other,
so tensile and swanlike in their stretch
that we could not look away.

Their bodies grew slick in the vertigo
of their vertical dance, and swiveling,
they looked and looked with the stalks
of their periscope eyes, little divining rods
electric with meaning.

Years later, with my tongue tracing
the areolas of your breasts, I follow the whorl
of the helix shell. I breathe the dank earth.
My earliest fancies rise within me,
and you take me back to the woods.

Eros:

the well-kissed fold in the belly;
     love
          (the verb)
               bouncy in its parentheses;
the giant squid's foot-wide eye
     mostly veiled from us,
and the idea of its eighth arm
          twining with another;
the thrill of restraint
          against desire,
     the anonymity of the caretaker
who will anoint us
          in our final bath;
the blindfold
     and the lightness of the hand
          on the small of our back.

The Anglerfish Finds her Muse

Tonight I wake as an anglerfish,
ringing my world with light,
prowling the window sill, gutted of flies,
the bedroom's shadowed amalgams and rifts,
its submarine and faceless blooms of mouths
and stomachs, waving tentacles and threads
that go trawling above the lure-light
that sprouts from my head,
the fatal charm that obscures me.
In a room of nose-diving lamps,
little twitching schools of fish, and you,
my broadside eyes obvert and roll inwards,
indrawn to a sleeping language,
where I am not a fish or a woman,
but the nocturnal verb
that brushes up between you and me,
legible in the curve of our dreaming.

The Glass Squid

Nearly unseen, so limpid
as to be lost, the glass squid
is a genius of minimalism;
even her outthrust eyes conceal their long shadows,
their undersides casting forth light as from street lamps
and effacing their structures.

The glass squid never outgrows
her competent transparence,
although I wonder if she feels quite safe
when she passes her predators: moiré chambers
with electric lures and waving, tentacled things
that shiver against seaweeds

or medusa heads, trawling
or still. Night is a fiction
below, yet the darkness that the diver
caught on camera could be in a Caravaggio.
There's a cost to see the squid's eyes tricked into sight;
her dark, broadside world was lit

for an instant not by light
of her design.   Was she scared?
Did she flee to seek a veil of seaweed?
And did the diver, armored and as riveted
as a lover, follow? The two would have traveled
to the deepest dark, where masked

eyes look as through a glass seal.
Those below survive with minds
that are semaphores of alarm, while some
must cope with a force—violent and vestigial—
that nests in neural readiness, quick to transmit
its misprision, as in love.

Zoo Dream

Below a vertical zoo, at the edge
of waking, I dream up a vast body
with a domed head, skin tougher than a tortoise's,
and I —in the new tenancy of my elephantness—
test my trunk, a casual pendulum

as precise as a dragonfly's landing,
and fan my ears like a lady shaking
out drapery. Propulsion begins, as it must,
with the idea of *mother*, my own— I know—is away,
lost or exiled from this place of exile

and I must find her (laws of early love
transpose us). Beneath the crush of my legs,
the stairs sway and buckle, and each landing carries
a mewling and baying. Still I tramp for miles, searching.
Soon I am a pure tug, a handler's dream.

Lonesome George:

the last member of the Chelonoidis abingdoni species
(circa 1912- 2012)

Probably the God of Tortoises,
with his bacteria-rich kiss
and his shell as wide as a barouche,
loves you, George.
He will be magisterial but clement,
welcoming; he will scoop his neck
across the vault of heaven and take you in,
his ponderous face upon yours.
He will jest with you,
take you for a lope across the shaded lawns.
Light will play on the intricate scutes
of his shell when he reminds you
that no animal goes unmolested on this earth,
and to be the last is to suffer idolatry
or worse, this mortal irony:
the zoo plans to embalm you
(because preservation, though tardy
at this juncture in your lineage,
is pressing for posterity's sake).
Someone will suture you,
mammoth and sloe-eyed,
with dust deep in the crevices of your skin
and the ancient minerals of the earth,
for the last time, cemented in.

The Last Animal

When we kill, we do it well.
I have paid to see their bones
encased in glass: rib cage,
incisors, broken femurs
suspended by wires. Skeletons
require care. Stuntwork. I've stroked
the memory of tortoise
in concrete parks, and loitered in halls
of heads and thrusting torsos.

When we kill, we do it well.
We strip the trees of music,
we miss the flowers, we forget
that metaphor is molecular.

When no one notes again
the inner tension of the crouching fox
before it vaults over the fence
or the hungry cat that enters a room,
tail swishing, to assert a mood,
who will notice the first signs of the suicidal?

Do not mistake me
killer, friend.

Family Circus

Here they come! we cry as one
when the handlers roll their cages up
from the stables in the basement.
A kid, sucking at his bars, wears a wig
of wool like a real goat,
and another licks and licks and licks
down her last fur until the ham of her leg
glistens pinkly.

But she can be stitched up
with a darning needle. Here live
the fables of mammals;
the pleasure of the lie is better
than companions. Better
than the accounting of the spirit.

An infant bird wheezes an anthem
across the sequined air,
and the redundant cannons do
what they do, and soon the kids
clamber in and play dumb
at the ringmaster's order.
He keeps them squinched in the butt end
of his universe, where they spoon his ramrod
until the countdown. And shot up
from the barrel, blood echoing in their ears,
they climb the sky like flares across a stolen sea.

Openly, the ringmaster loves his kids;
he tells us about love through the brass and whistles.
We love them too: hunchbacked or stunted,
broken in and funny looking.
They are cute or they are strange,
they make us laugh or tremble,
but now we must eat or piss,
and the ringmaster points us to the exit.

Sword Swallowing

To me, the work's consoling when they watch:
   I tilt my head and thread the saber down
my throat until—from hilt to point—the shaft's
   delivered deep inside the pharynx, tight
within the gullet. Edging close, the crowd
   regards my sternum, craving more: the live
and pendent-still taste of steel, the slit-eyed
   devourer's want, the sight of the blade
in darkness, pinned within the organs' coil
   of passageways and funnels. Art betrays
this need for intimate exchange; it thins
   the line between us, freaks and patrons all.
Agape, I ventilate the void inside:
   I body forth our wish to bypass flesh.

Mummified Baboon, Unburied

When they come for me, they come with shovels,
augers and picks. A cloth still holds dermis
to bone, but barely, and when they raise me
from an oven of hot sands to daylight,
I'm a dazzlement of husk. They lay out
my face, my hips, the undeveloped strip
of my spine, all turned to anthracite hues.
Their catalogue—bone by bone—deems me whole,
and, amassed and outlined against the earth,
I'm turned from corn doll to brittle city.
They map and flag my parts, then break me up
to store me. And later, I am encased
and placed on display. *What is this devotion?*
A child peers inside the glass and strains to find—
beneath some bindings—fellowship in death.
But my face is in tatters. Someone says,
It was preserved so its soul would live on
after death. The formula's miscarried,
though; it's a far more cryptic sapience
that saves me now. It's unguent and heat,
and years of subsoil basking that keeps me.
It is for these all too precious splinters
that I'm not received, but not forsaken.

The Condor

Why carp about her appetite?
Post-feast, she reels around the corpse
still inflected with flies and the ship-like,
collapsing ribs inverted in the sand.

And while she considers lift off
with her phalanx of dissectors
and feasters, she drowses, anchored—stranded—
by her own belly. Still, one admires

the homely extemporizer,
her dinosaur face and bald crown,
playing at the sinews of her chow,
which is considerable (an entire cow),

and bayoneting with her beak
the hide so as to scoop the pulp
and heart. Her vast hunger is not absurd,
but serviceable; living off her meal

for days, she's free of self-offense,
alert not to the guilt that trails
great need, but to the angles of her wings
and the winds that fan her collar of fringe.

Apropos a Tortoise

I.

Notes on a tortoise:
slumberous step, darting eye,
crown cross-hatched with age.

II.

He loses balance
and capsizes into wet
leaves; he's frond-flooded.

III.

Retreating, his head
backs into a chamber dark
with soft coiled flesh.

IV.

Hibernation starts
with fraying skin and spoiled
fruit; the days darken.

V.

The reptilian frame
bears the cracks of grandmother's
old cameo brooch.

VI.

I raise the emblem
of age to my face; the dark
inlaid mirror shifts.

Word Problem #3

A pair of tuataras play
I spy with my parietal eye
on the banks of a silt-lined river.
One, the mother, ogles
a winking firefly at twelve o'clock
with the vestige of its third eye,
while her kid lifts its baggy-neck
to the moon. They are content;
the weather is fine and no one cannibalizes
the other (an evolutionary faux pas
still passed down to the unlucky few).
Nonplussed as teenagers,
they wallow at the shallow's edge
and swish their little tails,
their scales catching the lights
of the universe like ancient mosaic tiles.

After millennia, their kind
is as inoculated against time
as angels. They have earned
the casual lives of golfers, and yet one day
man and his Maker arrive on the scene
to transport the two across the river.
The Maker, a kayaker (not much of a lifeguard),
is without illusions:
he can bring only one at a time
and if he leaves man alone
with either mother or kid,
man may kill one or the other.
Meanwhile, the Maker, without design,
cries, *How will they cross the river?*

All at Sea

I am not blameless
living off of my mother's belly.
I know my thirst
and I know my crimes.
I know yours.

But do you remember—in your dreams—
our emergent bodies ghosting below the sea line?
Remember how we learned from the stinging flowers,
the viruses, the cetacean songs
that echoed below the ice-sheeted earth?
I miss those songs still,
how we thrilled in somatic reply
from body to body, to wave after wave.

Do you remember the coastlines
and their riches before we branched forth limbs
and stood ashore, our infant knees trembling forth?
And can you dream her up as she was then
before our fatal bloom across her giving breast?

They say the sea is a mirror.
Look, and there we are:
a fluke, a dying kind. And our mother now?
She is there, shrunken, sagging,
shocked by our overhandling
and the banquet we hold across the spine
of her back.

Like you, I am a monster of desire,
and when I drink her in, I taste my grave.
I have maimed her to the core.
But her logic of mercy is neat:
when I thirst for the last time,
mother will be a yielding desert,
and I shall suck her bones dry.

II.

"[Representation] means that the real animal can disappear...The dog is a representation of the human; it is not, paradoxically, a dog."

—Erica Fudge, "A Left-Handed Blow"

Observations on the Ostrich: An Anti-Parable

Like a funerary fop,
the ostrich is bustle-plumed
and clergyman-hued, its raked up feathers
evincing couture, its pinched head setting
its saucer eyes in relief. In panic,

the ostrich flops to the earth
and flattens its sand-colored
head against the land to hide. Farther off,
the lion beholds stretches of desert
and a shrub or shadow rooted against

the landscape. Man, distant too,
sees an artless bird. He says,
That is the attitude of fear: the bulk
forgotten to save the head, stashed in sand.
Meanwhile, the poet, intent to capture

the beast, retreats in simile
and costumery to bare
the ostrich to the man, while the lion,
in the service of the poet's mission,
lies in the glimmer of her misprision.

Colossal Squid in Combat

They say the monster wrestles whales;
          clamping its tentacles around
                    one's back, its musculature pressed
against the blubber in grand sprawls
          of suckers, teeth, and whirling hooks,
                    its mass contorting in darkness,
it grants this compact of bodies
          recorded in Atlantic foam.
                    They've been glimpsed off Newfoundland's coast
grappling in slick embrace, although
          (here an annotation's fastened
                    to the tale) rarely do the pair
make of their tryst, meat. More often,
          interlinked (think of a chokehold's
                    precise architecture), they die
before victory, together,
          and drift across the floor, the way
                    furniture glides around a room
during a lifetime. In the end,
          the long-tottering leg will break
                    off the chair, the squid will dangle,
then drop away from its purchase,
          lacy with decay. Its endnote
                    will scuttle along the bottom

of the page, pedantic and vain.

Leda

Afterwards, pregnant,
she moved into a third floor apartment
and spent her cash on reprints.
And in them, the men,
the mythmakers, who heard her story
told in the bird's words,
turned her—in picture after picture—
into tragic furniture or
a doll-body draped
around the roundness of the god
of gods, whose extended neck
lanced across her belly
and pinned her under
a mountain of feathers.

While the creatures grew and dabbled
within her, she drew portraits of herself
not as woman or beast,
but as machine—
a windmill with lines as hard
as her jaw and blades spotlighted
with wind lines.
To be efficient, quotidian, intact—
not Dutch nor quixotic:
this was her wish.
Flowerless, her landscapes were filled
with fissures in the earth, outlines
of cliffs as broad as giant's legs,
and a narrow pass between them.

Forty days later, a twitching
and bustling inside the eggs
broke the spell of her sleep,
and she watched the creatures peck
and head-poke the encasings,
their progress slow,

more excruciating than exquisite.
She imagined all of them into existence:
chicks within a close-quartered mine,
tapping at the veins
where any light is a surprise
to newborn eyes and the slightest glint
might be the first sighting
of gold or an opening.

Ars Poetica

On the upbeat of her wings,
    the damselfly lifts off and tacks,
her aerial dip and swerve

        curving her towards the scrub
flanking the glinting river.
    You close in, the camera eye

jutting forth, fixed on the blade
    of a sedge plant where she rests,
her lateral wings stilled

        for an instant while you stand
over her, the birdwatcher's
        insect, the most photogenic

and challenging to catch
    on camera. Sharpening
the focus, you view the complex

        cross-veins traced along her wings
and the globes of her eyes
        bisected with bands of sky

and steel blue. Before you snap
    the shot, she, milling her wings,
skitters and darts to the cleft

        of a rock, the water moss,
the knob of an upended root,
        the papery veil of a lily.

You step forth to intercept her,
    but she—in her acrobatics— resists
your freezing eye, flourishing

        her gift for evasion.

Obstare

Armor clanks within.
          An acceder to the anterior,
ingrown, incubates
          in the iconic brow.
Somehow, a hammering
          sounds and strengthens
within the great swallower,
          the god of gods.
Host or daughter,
          his handiwork hunches,
leaden against his lobes,
          her lidless eyes
are trained towards his.
          Taking watch from behind
the ocular glass—
          offscreen, but omniscient—
she fathoms the visions
          of her father; they're inverted,
of course, seen
          sub rosa, from inside.
The headaches grow.
          When she hacks out of her hold,
splits head-first,
          she— sage—will sound
her birth-cry;
          bearing down to bear herself,
she'll broach not babyhood,
          but her bare-knuckled self
and her father's brain;
          her future will be a fight
to right and refocus
          that pre-filial film.

The Apocalypse Comes to Bodega Bay

It's the end of the world,
    Tippi Hendren is smoking a cigarette,
and from the schoolhouse the children are singing,
    The butter came out a grizzle-y-grey
Ristle-tee, rostle-tee, Now, now, now!

And while the crows file along the steel poles
    of the playground by twos, then tens,
the song circles and crests without reason,
    growing as grating and absurd
as Tippi's mink-coated complacency.

When they flee, the glossy bodies cling to their collars,
    aiming for the napes of their necks, their earlobes.
They clot the skies and rap through the walls:
    mechanical gulls, seabirds riveted to wires,
sparrows in hundreds shattering the laws of nature.

Never doubt the terror of a collective intelligence.
    In every apocalypse, the prophet is the local drunk,
and the girl is too beautiful and wild.
    Coppery Mitch with his bullet head is hankering
to tame her, then war against the omniscient birds.

Easter Dinner

First, there's the prayer over the roast;
both are tidy, greased with devotion.
God is at the table. Some wife is too,
and an overhandled infant girl,
who tries and tries to squirm out of reach,
but is always brought back to eat.
He sharpens his knives and carves the bird.
Later his teeth grind down on politics and gristle.
He prefers his meat to be soft as an ear lobe,
the wings and face avulsed from the body,
all traces of her life and death
dismembered from the table.

Someone could recall the bird before
when she nipped ice crystals out of her wings
and sunbathed at dawn. Or someone
might speak of how she sang her horror through blood
when they shackled her legs,
hung her upside down, and slit her throat,
cutting her head clean off. But no one does.
In time, he will leave the table
to colonize a TV chair and nod off,
and the wife, humming to herself,
will clear the carnage from the table.
The night will come, the Resurrection will pass,
and all of her life the infant with her overlarge eyes
will carry a hunger in her belly
for something else.

The Display

I.
Gone: the lilac dive,
the glitter of pollen. Gone
too are the cosmos.

II.
Bestowed on a tack,
below the thorax, the name
Papilio hovers.

III.
The grave enclosure
frames the line-up: they're tagged now,
stiff in their lockup.

IV.
Mounted, splayed like cards,
the Pieridae are flightless;
just cut up play-hearts.

V.
Moths, their negatives,
are over-exposed, their scales
like gauze in bulbed light.

VI.
The voyeur eye frets
at their flourished laterals,
their backs gripped by pins.

V.
Not stomped on, nor swept
away, these bugs, with pupil-
patterned wings, stare back.

For a Frog

Caged, at home in a glassed country,
you, basker, take to the walls,
balled into the angle of penitence:
eyes lidded, asparagus-limbs tucked in,
pointillist belly on display—
just a thumbnail thing mosaicked

and edged with larvae eggs, planets,
and marbled fleas. I could mistake
the belly for map, the frog for token
or decor: a pellucid brooch, maybe,
or worse— a captive of my need,
a prince tricked into compression

or cipher for all overlooked
and misperceived things. You're equal
to my mishandled love, my delicate
and hard-to-keep creature, whose mood matches
all the species of forest green
and swaps their shades to stay intact.

Your belly though is a worry;
the fine, visible tracery
of your tract is a debacle
of translucence. When you misread your leap
and land, little filament-legs readied,
I dive and clutch, scaring you
into zones beyond human reach.

The Elephant Shrew

is neither elephant nor shrew, but could be called
epicure-insectivore or—more to the point—
termite-guzzler for her taste in drywood squatters
which, in anteater fashion, she flicks in her mouth
with her tongue. Misnomer, she roams the driest steppes
of southern Africa, hopping on spindle legs
and twitching her elephant nose en miniature
like a rabbit, though she is more compact, with ears
papyrus-thin and eyes ringed with white to set off
an astonished look, fitting for the one Adam
misnamed, whose identity slips from language's pin.

Classifieds:
Missed Connections

I.

At every estuary I ask for you.
We had a laugh wading near the mangroves,
waiting for the sun to come up.
You were a pink lamp in the dawn,
a rococo pink, with a body contoured like a heron
and feathers bunched up
like flounce on a flamenco dress.
In our stretch of swamp, silhouetted tortoises
slid past us, a speck of regret in their eyes,
and you found a little knot of fish
to spoon up with your spatula bill,
trilling a riff of bullfrog-grunts
and surfacing with your mouth
fringed with fronds.
In spring, I will be skimming
across the lower latitudes,
looking out for you. Let's not worry
about probability or the weather.
If you read this, what is the weather to us?

II.

With the eggshell tiling of your belly draped in mud
and your immaculate scales glinting like ceramic in the sun,
you lolled (strategically?) near me, your tail,
articulate and comely, sweeping half moons
along the swamp bank. You smelled of dropworth
and mouldering larvae, and I blew networks of clinging,
bottle green bubbles across your cheeks.
You showed off your snout and curled your forelimbs
around mine; for a full minute, you and I were entwined.

III.

I saw you blinking your wings
against the marine green finish
of a gas pressure lantern.
Pheromones and kerosene spiked
the air, and I flitted above your thorax,
stuttering against your sparked
fury (you had browned your wings
from the light, usually a yucca white).
We found dusty moth wings
pressed like flower petals
along the lantern rim, and we bolted,
returning to the moon as our frame of reference,
and beating wings as thin as confetti
against the night. Although for you,
I would balance astride the flame's eye
and meet a night swelling with lanterns.

Word of the Day: **Mutt** [muht]

Noun *Slang*
1. a mongrel dog; cur
2. a stupid, ignorant, or foolish person
3. an ugly, disliked girl
4. a term of contempt for a biracial person

Word Origin and History: A Personal Account

1992, mother-"A mutt is a mixed breed, like Mr. Richardson's dog."

1993, a beanpole kid with a mean face- "Your cousin is a mutt."

1993, mutt- a sting, a word that makes mother angry; a feeling of falling, my body helicoptoring down and down and down like a seedpod streaking off its hook; a livid red flush on my face; my cousin's voice in the next room, and my mother's whispered voice: "a bad word."

2013, mutt- a memory of my cousin standing before the amaryllis bush, laughing before our *race*, when race meant a run from the front porch to the very edge of our yard and back; a semaphoric shock from the ear to the chest, when our blood sluices through the arteries to gird our hearts, their pump slackening to a thin sob.

If I Were Your Sister and You Were a Bird and All the Wolves Were Buried and Dead

For Jessie

Color me blue and red, I said, and you filled in
my face purple, your paints spilling over
the lines. An only child no more,
I took to the flung-togetherness of our lives:
the way my comebacks bled into your repartee,
the winter days I'd find your mitten coupled with mine,
the new territories of care and fury between us,
more sisters than cousins. You the *Polo to my Marco*,
the blindman to my bluff. If you hid
I would follow. All day we would backfloat
angels into the first snowfall, and when I blended in,
you called me white as snow. But our mothers
couldn't miss us. Each morning mine
or yours would grab one of us and tug a pick
through your baby afro or my baby knots
before we struck out for school, sidling into seats
at the back of the bus. But the phrase meant nothing
to us then but a spot away from prying eyes;
it was not a command or the state of the race.
Besides, I was a zebra fish or something
very much like it, and you were a catbird,
and we didn't know anything about the need
to call ourselves one thing or another.
But maybe the bluff was yours,
and all that time—between playing pranks
and dress up, making dares and taking them—
you knew that wolves—real ones— stalked the city blocks,
and while I could blend in, you cut your teeth
when one caught sight of your skin
and I blindly walked on to a different street.

The Monster Underfoot,

the one like a secret
calcified below the sea
with its doughy face blanched
and flecked with bruise- pinks,
studded with mossy warts,
and razor-spines stocked with venom,
is not a monster, but a stonefish.

But it is monstrous
to be like stone, they say,
if you are not a stone.

They say it has a fringed underlip
thick with seaweed,
guts as lumpy as a busted tire
and a body that is like stone,
but not.

I am not stone or monster,
or even the fish underfoot,
the one darting in and out of the stones,
half-glimpsed beneath the wharf abloom
with rough-petaled barnacles,
but the slippage in sight,
the flash of the current
between fish and stone.

III.

"In trying to reveal the clash of elements that we are—the intellectual, the animal; the blunt, the ingenious; the impudent, the imaginative—one dare not be dogmatic. We are a many-foliaged tree against the moon; a wave penetrated by the sun."

—Marianne Moore, <u>Prose</u>

Eventually Iguanas,

with their spines and jowls
and their topographic backs
would move her, but first and forever were the turtles.
So protected, those nerve cords
in their bodies. Their bodies in their shells.
She loved their bird-beaks,
their pledge to the shadowiest places,
their powers of self-retraction.
They were the origins of her dreams,
as were the spittle bugs, the stars,
the misfits and the spiral flowers, the curl
of the fiddlehead ferns, the satin bowerbirds'
mania for blue.

She too was an elusive blue
heron, gecko-eyed and back-glancing,
who wrote elegies to the elephants
and heard military jets so loud
she could feel the reverb in her soul.
The world was heating up,
and rats as powerful as gods
thrashed about; they gnawed up her belly.
What could she do?
She ate nasturtiums with the turtles
to fill her.

The Seals off the Coast of Manomet

We came upon the colloquy of seals,
effusive in their idiom of barks and coughs.
Some speak with an inquisitive inflection
as if to ask, *How does this relate*
to what we were talking about?

And how do we respond in turn
to these creatures draped and lolling
along the razor-edged rocks,
their skin lustrous in the damp air,
while others stipple the distance

with their bobbing heads?
They shimmy off the ledges
when they see us or are phlegmatic
and sloe-eyed, like a Degas nude
in her chaise lounge. One bull heaves

a belly as big as a kettle drum
up onto a slab, his neck receding
into the wrinkles of his scarved fat
as he bellows to us, probing our reasoning:
How could these marvels be refuted?

The Mimic Octopus,

Merceau-like, flaunts the exact art
> of mirroring one's match. Part mime,
part ham (though not to predators),
>> it can approximate the state

of a curled sea anemone
> if an enemy gives it chase,
extending its faux tentacles
>> coquettishly, as if to tease

or transfuse poison. Down below,
> relation is forged in instants,
and it must shed the self swiftly
>> to become a foe: an army

of flowering snakes or a ray's
> alter ego. With its body
embodying the other,
>> it finds itself safest in acts

of correspondence: the traffic
> in identity, the sudden
incipience of encounter,
>> when a signal gives birth to form.

The Man Born with a Snake Heart

"Atavism is the rare reappearance, in a modern organism, of a trait from a distant evolutionary ancestor. We describe an apparent case of atavism involving a 59-year-old man with chest pain whose coronary circulation and myocardial architecture resembled those of the reptilian heart."

-"A Case of Atavism in a Human Being": Abstract

Before the twinge and pain in his chest,
there were the dreams: scenes of wetlands
flooded with milkweed and cattail,
sulfur rank in the air, and mudflats
where he thrilled in secret at the sight
of a frog, wall-eyed and refulgent
beneath a sheen of bog water.

And he dreamed of his wraparound self,
bound around the bough of a hemlock
before shuddering off a ribbon of skin,
moulting a thin ghost of himself to be lost
in the rustle of leaves. He drowses
under a copse or tests the wiry
alacrity of his body, fluent as a fist.

Later, with his chest tricked out with electrodes
and jelly-slick with a robin blue luster,
he watches the shivery green pulsation
of his heart on the monitor, while the echo
gives voice to its liquid beating,
and belly-up, he hears with his whole being
the oblique, blubbery throb of god's ruse.

Questions for an Ornate Wobbegong

On some nights, in a fugue,
you feel a sudden glassiness
obtrude upon the objects of your world.
You thumb the avocado spine
of a book or the pulp of berries
in their square bowl. Then you glance
in the mirror, and the dog
you don't own
gives you bunny ears from behind.

What about the ornate wobbegong,
a carpet shark with a blunt jacquard snout
and a slightly toadish face
abloom with seaweed-like stalks,
whose body so matches her world
that divers mistake her for coral and fronds
tangled on the floor of the western Pacific?

Does she ever glimpse her whiskered mug
in the reflection of a diver's mask
and wonder if she is observing flora and reef,
and then— with creeping horror—
see a self, secreted in a crevice?

The Lioness

After the attackers leave, the lioness
finds her cub, splayed and half-gone.
She laps at his face, his breast, his haunches
with the shivery pink tip of her tongue,
mouths the crown in the O of her jaws.
She works her tongue through the lush jungle
of his veins, plucks at the muscle,
thin as violin strings,
swills the blood, grinds the fat,
sucks from the wreck
of his bones until they glint like stars,
until she eases him back into her.
Above, the vultures wait then flag, thwarted.
In the economies of death,
let there be no waste,
and if there is a witness overhead,
let my body's strange devotions deter him.

Every Little Elegy I Finish

steers me farther away from you.
Now I write about the aggravated gulls
and the whales, imprisoned in their bulk,

who have been beached ashore
and cannot shy away from our ministrations
while the tide is pulled out.

Soon the moon is cleared away like a dish,
and the tide goes out with the whales' song;
it carries past the dunes and soda joint,

and past a set of shapeless curtains
behind which a lady sloshes into a bath's hot froth.
The vibrations begin against the porcelain,

and channel up her spine
to the ear canal. Her brain picks up
the accent of a dying tongue,

amplified by the tub's dimensions,
but far too distant
and visceral for translation.

When the Horseshoe Crab Grieves

Dying, I confide in starfish and lightning.
The stones, twittering distantly, speak to me.
The rain in our open graves is a temporary relief,
and from underneath the echo chamber
of my shell I hear a soft moaning
and dream of the new moon I cannot see.
We speak of the flung-togetherness
of our lives: how the slapping tide
can turn us like dice and the fish nets
frilled with carrion-strings bind us:
translucent lobes of jellyfish, dangling crabs,
and twisted cordage of seaweed.
All of us know the swift feedback
of pain, even the armored ones like me.

Now the gulls that would knock all day
against the steel pan of my carapace
hesitate and watch from their priestly angle.
We are all poison and poisoned, slick with oil
and its rings of dark pearl.
I wear a black veil of seaweed.
Flies, those thieves of blood,
do not know to stay away.
Everywhere along the shore we cry for love
and the sweeping arms of a green sea.

The Ruse of Melancholy

is that it is without defenses,
like the wet dog turned back outdoors
or the tender parts of the soft shell turtle
with its back as exposed as a soft belly.
I want to think that the dry underbelly of the deck
or the riverbank sludge provides a permanent mantle.
Beneath the shed of you, I am happy,
afraid to look out.

The Venus Girdle

When passion was the plaything of the gods,
the epithet spelled Eros,
the girdle magicking love among mortals.
In desire, though, we need no devices
to remake ourselves.
Desire is the creature below:
it has no hook or eye closures
nor was en vogue with the winged bicycle,
but is instead alive, an aquatic hermaphrodite
that has no need to cinch its waist
as it winds snakelike around seals and eels below.
Slight, almost immaterial,
it could be mistaken for a crimp
in the mid-Atlantic, a secret seen slantwise
that turns luminous at night
and ribbons through the waters
close to the surface.
Tricked out with rows of combs,
it is the queen of jellies;
it teaches us the etiquette of love—
all the customs by which we are riven.

Domestic Tortoise

I can intuit now the initial stutter forward
towards the sunlit carpet, the rest and rapt attention,
the pebbled back glinting beneath the window.
Do you like my world, what it yields?
The morning bowl of blueberries, the music,
the scum-lined aquarium, the curtained moonlight,
the plastic water dish? Despite this safety,
I cannot excise the rhythms of fear and retreat in your step.
And the earth may miss you, your darting eye,
your adorable fastidiousness around carrots,
and the slant of your neck,
your face turned away from mine.

Nursery Web Spider

My mother ferries me in her fangs,
then in her palps, until hatching time.
In an otherworld, tucked away
in a tumbledown room,
she begins her involved labor;
from her spinnerets she invents
arcane glyphs, reticulate and comely,
and entwines a nursery tent in the skeins
of her web. The outer loops, edged with flies,
do not distract her: she slips the egg sacs
into a silk cradle, then stands as sentry
until the day I emerge as a spiderling
and—drawn forth as if by an invisible bell—
I leave. I do not linger at the chink in the lintel.
I do not look back.

When I rappel off my dragline thread,
catch the first air draft, and balloon away,
I give over to the wind
and fly for months, miles
beyond her eight eyes
and the world of her making.

I could land anywhere, and I do:
far out at sea on a tall ship,
caught within a wide apron of sail.
My threads string across the atmosphere:
they lead me back to her.

When the Outdoor Cats Come In

Inside, we comment on her set
of leek green eyes
transfixed at a point,
her whiskery intelligence,
and her ears curving
like satellite dishes.
And when we miss
our male cat's mute entry,
she smells the day
imported on his coat:
the tinned fish
that was his breakfast
and the bird heart
that pulsed two beats
in his throat. She knows
he drowsed among the leaves
raked against the wattle fence,
atop the woolen socks
drying in the mud room,
and in the lap of my lover,
whose scent, I know,
has a splash of lavender,
a hint of coffee, and something else
I can't name that fills me
each time with a rush
of cardinal reds,
the musk of an underwing,
then a flock of colors hotter
than the reddest planet.

King of Saxony Bird of Paradise

Canary-chested,
with the black cape
of my back feathers raked up,
I raise from my brow
two plumes
colored enamel blue,
ribbon-thin and ridged
with queer, serial flags,
and swerve them
towards you,
    so far away,

and I—in the riot of my outflung love—
dance along the coiled vines,

   swinging

as if on the surface of the sun
and singing so as to relay
across radio frequencies
and migration routes
my whirring call
to you.

The Queer Creatures that Rise at Dusk

Out of her burrow,
        the long-eared hedgehog girl,
to get her girl, comes at dusk,
        wobbling along the cooling sands
        to find her lover,

compact and flac-soled,
        with a pinprick mole
on her chin. With others, she pulls herself
        in like a drawstring, but the long-eared girl
        draws her out,

and her back, once quilled
        and bristling, the size
of an enlarged heart,
        relaxes, growing as soft-textured
        as a doll's brush.

When they meet,
        their foreplay is gentle;
each takes turns sliding
        their back beneath the belly
        of the other;

they nip at their spines
        and rub their snouts
along their warm fur,
        anointed in musk
        and sweet tufted grass.

Dream of the Mid-Wife

You come to me in confinement,
bearing sponge and pail and a sliced open
pomegranate that spills
down your hand. I am naked,
and my lungs are being wrung
like wet laundry. You tell me
to breathe with you, and I do.
The pail's left beneath me,
To catch the blood, you say,
while you soap your hands
then squeeze the fruit
down my gullet. I lap at the juice.
You lift me closer and I fan open
like a touch-me-not, while you,
laughing, fold your hands inside,
soft moth wings probing,
and, reaching deeper,
thumb the cervix, palming
the tender, entwined life inside.
Come, cross-over, you murmur.
My lungs relax, and the globe
you rotate is righted.
Then, a creature with an oyster-
luster, as slippery as a fish,
crowns, cries, and pulls
away. She lurches outside,
then—finding her legs—takes off,
bucking through the yard.
You take my arm, and lured,
we follow; she might take us back

to that land of florid beasts
who have no baseline for love
or what forms love brings forth.

The Fish beneath the Portuguese Man of War

Although the inverted crown
squiring snarls of tentacles laced with poison

trawls for prey and goes winding, winding
down into the gloom like Escher stairs,

I flutter beneath the curtain
of stingers, riskless to me.

Tide-thrust polyps propel me forward,
like stewards of my will,

and I trail their colony— not a self—
that balloons an amethyst bladder above the sea line

while the tentacled clan goes fishing,
hovering like fringe around my fins.

In sleep, safe in the perimeter of their reach,
I drift eastwards, following a gas-filled moon.

Acknowledgements:

It is with grateful acknowledgement that I wish to recognize the editors of the following journals:

The Missouri Review: "All at Sea;" "What I Mean When I Say I Knew You Long Before We Met;" "Nursery Web Spider;" "Lullaby for Cat" and "Dream of the Mid-Wife"

Tupelo Quarterly Press: "The Last Animal" and "Zoo Dream"

Crazyhorse: "The Mimic Octopus"

The Baltimore Review: "The Condor"

Copper Nickel: "The Fish beneath the Portuguese Man of War;" "The Decorator Crab;" "The Glass Squid"

Verse Daily: "The Decorator Crab"

Ninth Letter: "The Queer Creatures that Rise at Dusk" and "Mummified Baboon, Unburied"

Stone Canoe: "When the Outdoor Cats Come In" and "Observations on the Ostrich"

Blackbird: "Eros" and "Leda"

Sixfold: "The Man Born with a Snake Heart"; "The Lioness"; "Missed Connections"; "The Anglerfish Finds her Muse"; "The Seals off the Coast of Manomet"

Canary: A Literary Journal of the Environmental Crisis: "Lonesome George"

Thrush Poetry Journal: "The Apocalypse Comes to Bodega Bay"

Linebreak: "To the Meerkat"

Barzakh: "Colossal Squid in Combat"; "For a Frog"

Unsplendid: "Obstare"

AbleMuse: "Sword Swallowing"

The New Formalist: "The Display"

Permafrost: "When the Horseshoe Crab Grieves;" "Eventually Iguanas"; "If I Were Your Sister and You Were a Bird and All the Wolves Were Buried and Dead"

Flyway: Journal of Writing and Environment: "The Elephant Shrew"

Prairie Schooner: "Easter Dinner"

I am deeply grateful to my teachers for giving me a map to a greener place, most especially Eric Keenaghan, jil hanifan, Tomas Urayoán Noel, and Laura Wilder. Thank you to Julie Gutmann, Therese Broderick, and Elizabeth Gordon for providing invaluable feedback and a weekly refuge for poetry. To my parents, for their love. And to Elise, my hedgehog girl: thanks for drawing me out.

About the Author:

Sarah Giragosian's poems have appeared in such journals as *Ecotone, Prairie Schooner, Baltimore Review,* and *The Missouri Review,* among others. She teaches in the department of Writing and Critical Inquiry at the University at Albany-SUNY.

Praise for *Queer Fish* by Sarah Giragosian:

Queer Fish is an original and daring book, crossing the boundaries between human and animal realms to transport us into the world of natural wonders where the poetry of deeply felt sensory experience is the key to inner truth. In this book of stunning metamorphoses, written with both precision and exuberant abundance, the conventional hierarchies disappear, and we are called upon to rejoice in our affinities with a horseshoe crab, an anglerfish, a condor, a tortoise, a damselfly, and squid. Intricately crafted and shrewdly observed, her poetry is participatory, coaxing readers to acknowledge their potential for both love and empathy: "tonight I wake as an anglerfish, / ringing my world with light" ("The Anglerfish Finds her Muse") and for hate and destruction: "We are all poison and poisoned / slick with oil / and its rings of dark pearl" ("When a Horseshoe Crab Grieves"). In this anti-fable world, animals discard their merely symbolic nature and become true agents, inviting us, human creatures, into dialogue and communion with them. These encounters redefine the poetics of Eros, as the scientific blends with the magical, the mundane with the eccentric, and a human lover can inhabit the "hermaphroditic soul / of love" or become "the long-eared hedgehog girl." The poet, like "The Decorator Crab," is an eclectic collector of nature's ordinary miracles, but is also a creature being collected by other creatures – immortalized, loved and accused by the chorus of voices that usher us into the world of mysterious and joyful correspondences between human and nonhuman.
—**Lucyna Prostko** *Infinite Beginnings* (Bright Hill Press, 2009)

With curiosity and wonder, Sarah Giragosian deftly crafts enchanting lyrics of menageries and memories, of mimic octopi and ostriches. Marianne Moore allegorized through pangolins and paper nautiluses. Elizabeth Bishop interrupted the world in the strange gaze of a seal staring up from the bay, near the fish houses. Whether recalling girlhood memories of snails mating in the woods or imagining swimming beneath Portuguese men of war's tentacles, *Queer Fish* pays loving attention to the honest signals all of life emits. These poems double for those calls, drawing us outside ourselves toward queerer imaginaries and more expansive intimacies.
—**Eric Keenaghan**, *Queering Cold War Poetry: Ethics of Vulnerability in Cuba and the United States* (Ohio State University Press, 2009)